A
Bat/Bar
Mitzvah
Journal

This is a journal for you to write in and enjoy at your leisure. It will not only serve as a way of capturing and recording the exciting times and meaning of your Bat/Bar Mitzvah, but will also be a memorable keepsake you will enjoy rereading in the future.

WRITTEN BY LINDA SCHWARTZ
ILLUSTRATED BY BEVERLY ARMSTRONG

Typesetting and Editorial Production: Kimberley A. Clark

ABOUT ME

My Hebrew name is _____

I'm named after _____

I was born on _____
month-day-year

I was born in _____
city, state

I now live at _____

There are _____ people in my family including me. They are:

_____   _____

_____   _____

_____   _____

_____   _____

A SELF-PORTRAIT

This drawing shows me as I now see myself.

I drew this picture on _____ when I was _____ years old.
                              month-day-year

I think my best feature is _____

People say I look a lot like _____

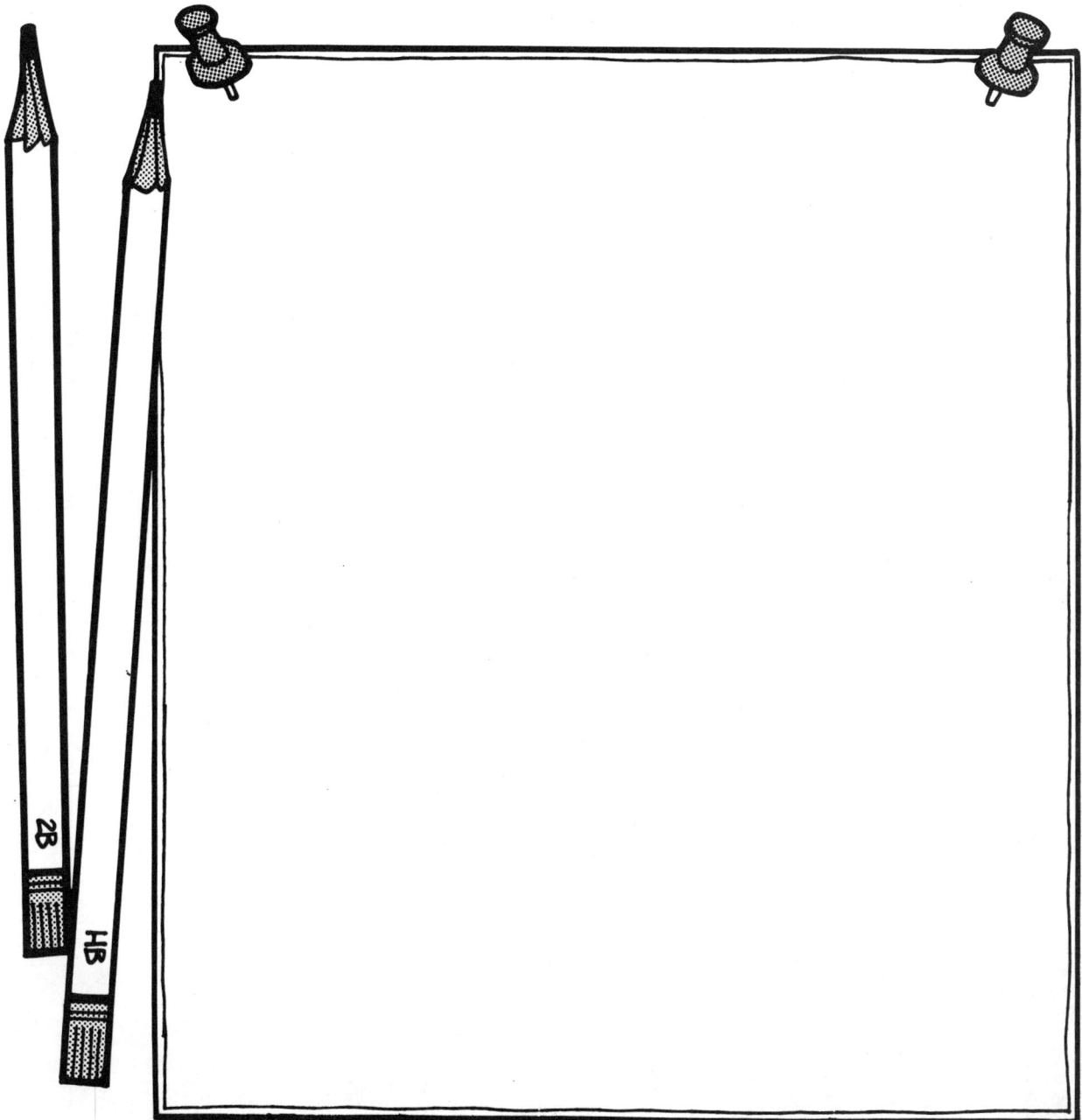

A POSTER OF ME

Look through magazines and find pictures and/or words that describe you. Cut them out and glue them in the space below.

jog   laughing   3 DOGS !   friendly

FOSSILS   PUMPKIN PIE   skateboard

TROMBONE   SOCCER   CHESS CLUB

gumdrops   casual   RAVIOLI

FANTASTIC FAVORITES

book _____

magazine _____

section of the newspaper _____

sport _____

game _____

video game _____

television show _____

movie _____

video _____

actor _____

actress _____

CD _____

recording group _____

things to wear _____

foods _____

things to do in my spare time _____

_____

THINGS I WISH
I COULD LIVE WITHOUT

essay TESTS
braces
REPORT CARDS
PHONE BILLS
broccoli
smog

EARTHQUAKES
ALARM CLOCKS
POISON IVY MOLD
HOMEWORK
MUD

zucchini
MOSQUITO BITES
FLU SHOTS
acne QUIZZES TAX
LIVER pain OKRA SLUGS
WEEDS

IF I COULD

If I could be any person in the world, I would be _____

because _____

If I could live during any period of history, I would choose _____

_____

If I could make one great discovery for the world, it would be _____

because _____

If I could have any talent I wanted, I would choose _____

because _____

If I could make one wish for the world, it would be _____

because _____

_____

ORIGINAL CREATIONS

ART

CREATIVE WRITING

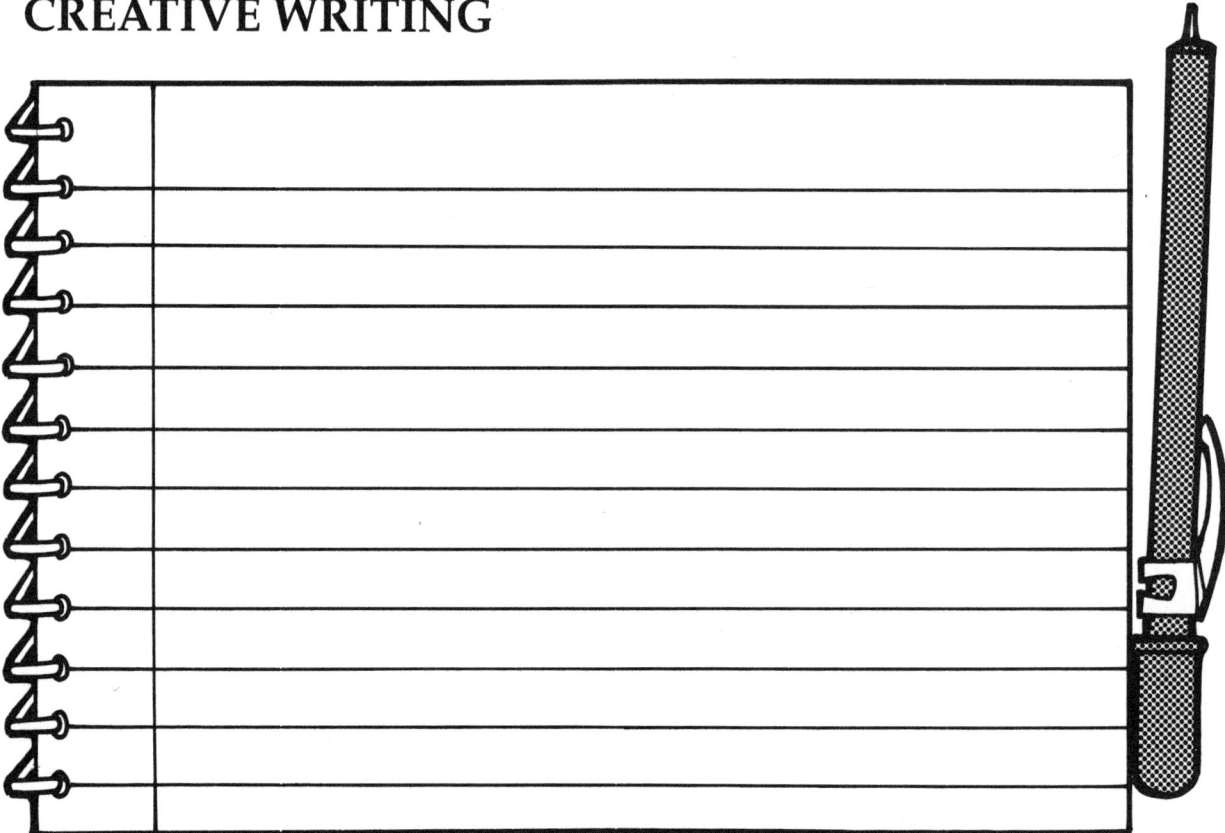

LIFE ON CAMPUS

I am in the _____ grade at _____ School.

My favorite subjects in school are _____

_____

My worst subjects in school are _____

_____

My favorite teachers are _____

_____

I belong to these teams, clubs, or special groups: _____

_____

Here is a schedule of my classes and teachers:

HEBREW EDUCATION

I've been going to religious school since _____

_____

I attend _____

name of temple or religious school

The names of my teachers are _____

_____

The part I like most about learning Hebrew is _____

_____

One of the most interesting things I've learned in Hebrew class is _____

_____

_____

Special classes I've taken or preparations I've made this year are _____

_____

_____

_____

MY THOUGHTS

ABOUT BEING JEWISH

ABOUT THE TORAH

ABOUT ISRAEL

MY THOUGHTS

ABOUT SABBATH

ABOUT MITZVOT

OTHER THOUGHTS

THE MEANING OF
BAT/BAR MITZVAH

As my Bat/Bar Mitzvah day approaches, here are some of my thoughts and feelings about what it really means to me:

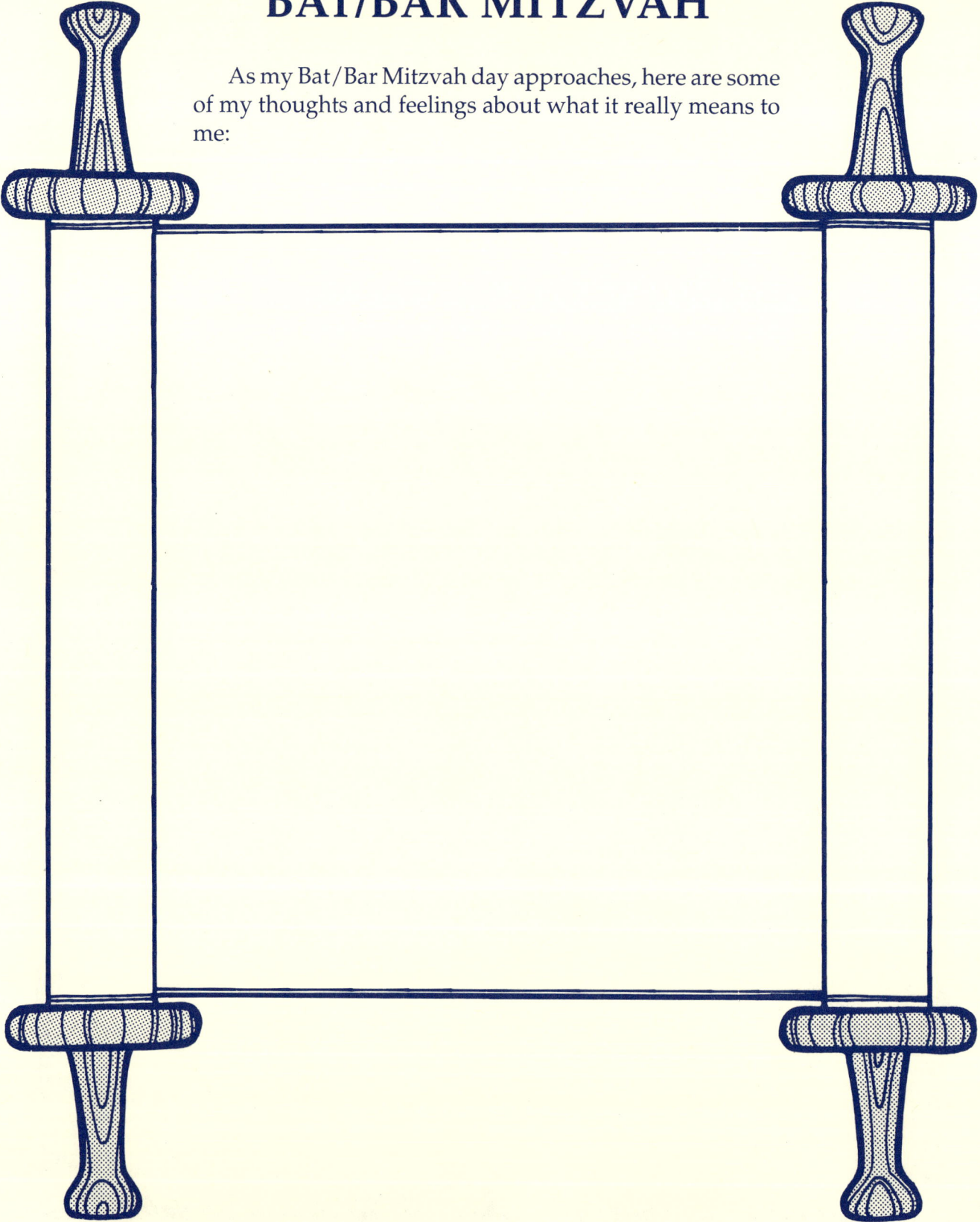

HIGHLIGHTS OF MY LIFE

Best childhood memory

Best trip or family vacation

Greatest accomplishment

Best thing that ever happened

TOP TRENDS

Record the things that are popular around the time of your Bat/Bar Mitzvah. You'll have fun comparing trends when you read this journal in the years to come.

Best-selling books

Popular movies

Top compact discs

Popular dances

Clothing fads

Kids' hairstyles

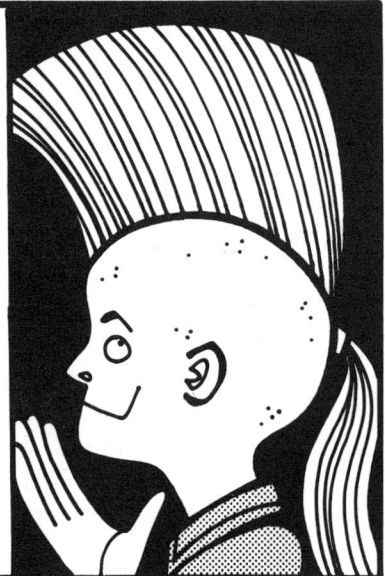

Top rock groups

Best computer games

Latest inventions

Favorite eating places

Top television shows

Games my friends and I enjoy

FAMILY ALBUM

Use this special time in your life to learn more about your family tree. Ask your mom or dad to tell you interesting stories about your grandparents, great-grandparents, aunts, uncles, cousins, and other relatives. In each space below, write the name of a relative you just learned about.

a relative who liked the same things I do _____

someone in the family I look like _____
name of relative

A funny incident was when _____

_____

_____

_____

I was surprised to learn that _____
name of relative

_____

_____

_____

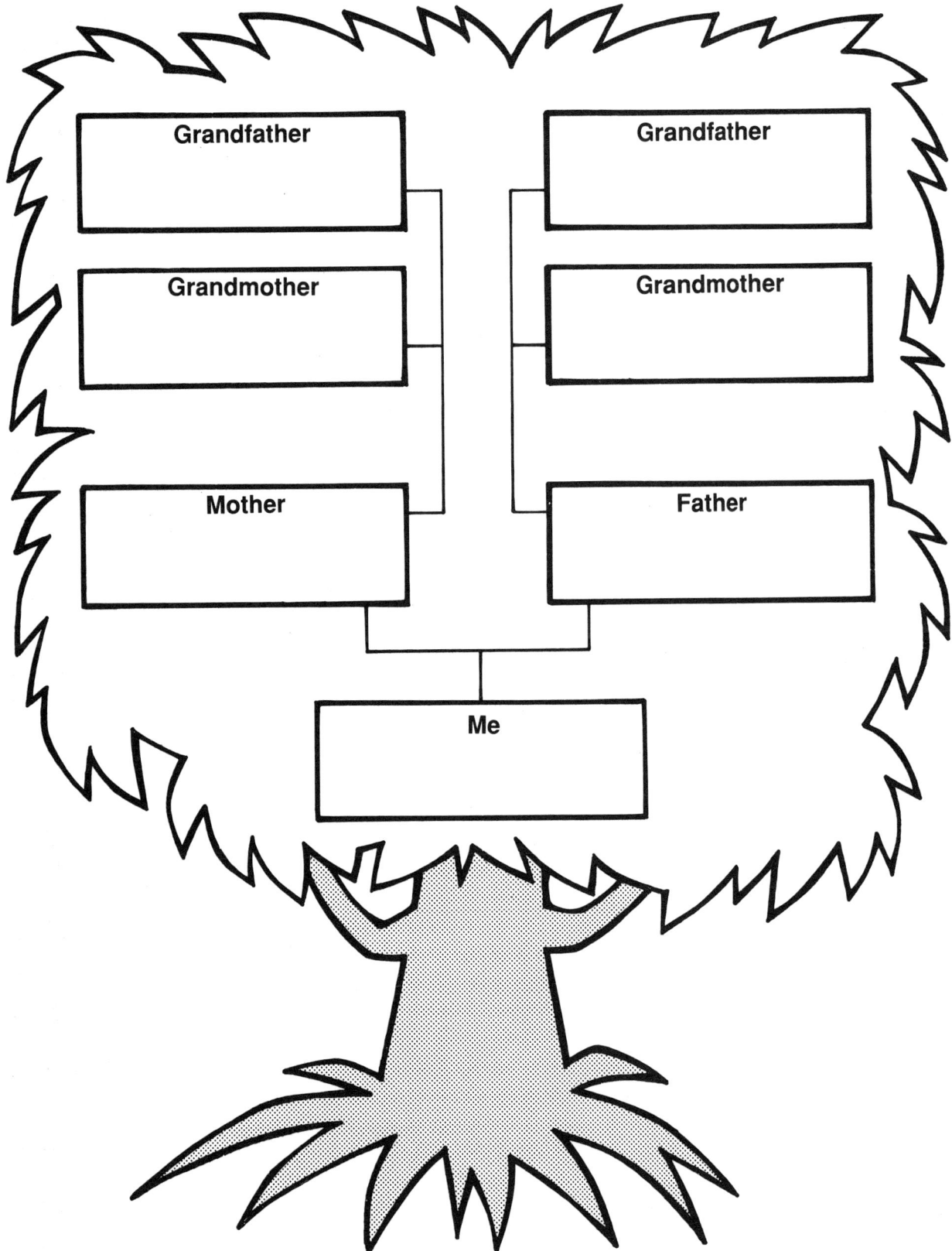

FAMILY TREE

Grandfather	Grandfather
Grandmother	Grandmother
Mother	Father

Me

ABOUT MY
BAT/BAR MITZVAH SERVICE

My Bat/Bar Mitzvah service took place on

_____
date

at _____
location

Services started at _____ o'clock

I began my part of the service at _____
time

My rabbi's name is

_____

My cantor's name is

_____

Special relatives and friends who attended:

_____   _____

_____   _____

_____   _____

_____   _____

_____   _____

_____   _____

ABOUT MY GUESTS

We had _____ guests at the service when I became a Bat/Bar Mitzvah.

Here are the names of some special guests:

the youngest_____ age _____

the oldest_____ age _____

traveled the longest distance _____

traveled the shortest distance _____

laughed the most _____

cried the most _____

danced the most _____

Fill in numbers for how many times guests said:

| "My how you've grown!"

| "Are you ready?"

| "Are you nervous?"

| "You did a fantastic job!"

| "Mazel Tov!"

MY INVITATION

Here is a sample of the invitation
we mailed to our guests.

THE BIG DAY AT LAST

This is what I wore
to the service:

This is what I did
to feel special:

Things I remember about people at the service:

MOM

DAD

BROTHERS/SISTERS

RELATIVES

FRIENDS

SPECIAL FEELINGS

On the morning of my special day, I felt

Once services actually began, I

The easiest part for me was

The hardest part for me was

During the service, I remember feeling

SPECIAL FEELINGS

I can recall looking out into the congregation and feeling

When I looked at my family, I

When I finished, I felt

I was surprised that I

If I had it to do all over again, I

I was proud of myself because

MY TORAH PORTION
AND HAFTARAH

My haftarah was _____

My Torah portion was _____

Here is a brief summary in my own words describing the Torah portion
and haftarah I read during services:

MY SPEECH

Here is the speech I gave following the reading of the haftarah.

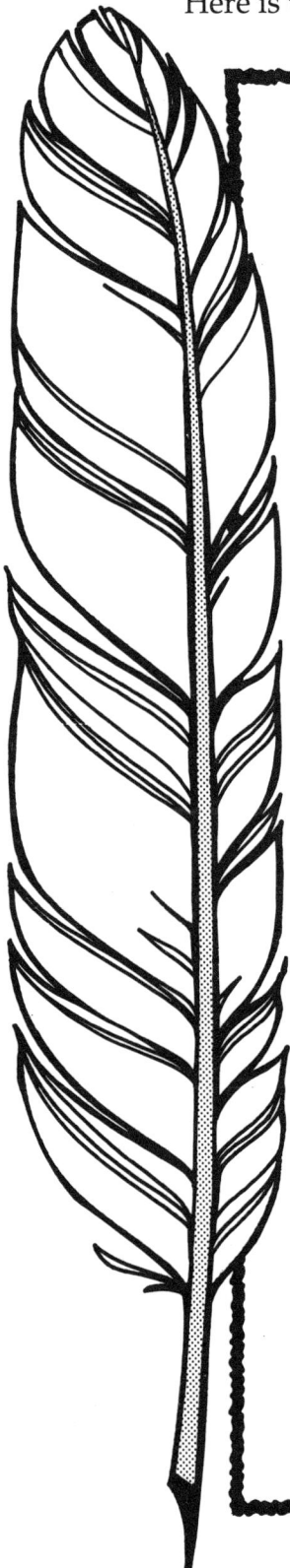

ALIYOT

The following people were called to the Torah
for aliyot during the service.

Name	Relationship
_____	_____
_____	_____
_____	_____
_____	_____
_____	_____
_____	_____
_____	_____
_____	_____
_____	_____
_____	_____
_____	_____
_____	_____

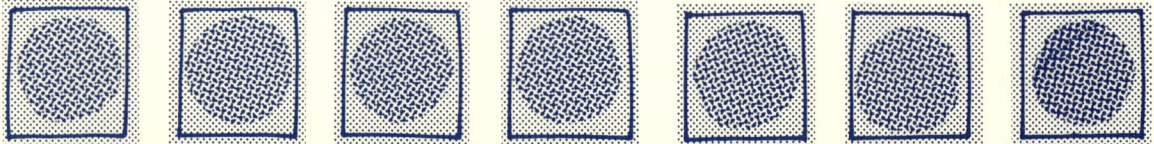

THE CELEBRATION

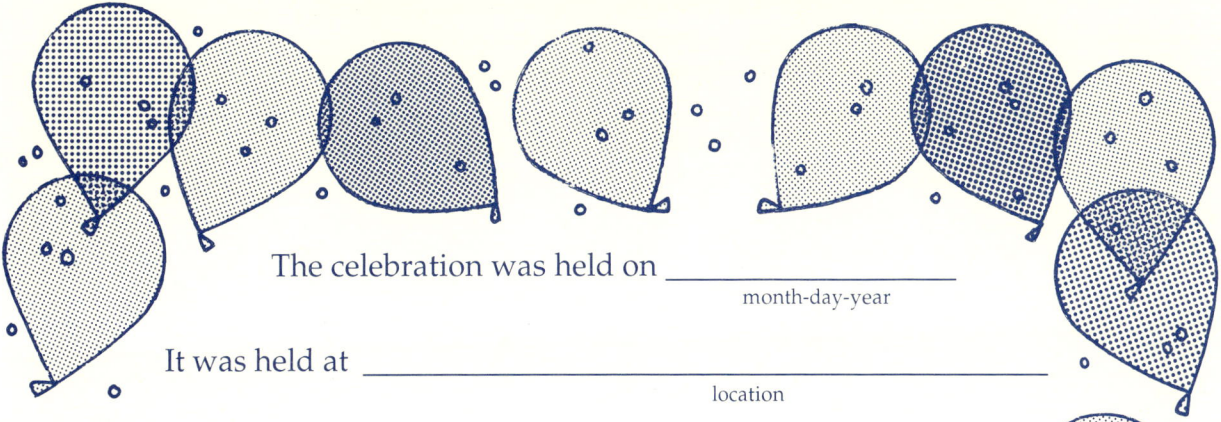

The celebration was held on _____
month-day-year

It was held at _____
location

at _____ o'clock.

There were about _____ people at my celebration.

CELEBRATION MEMORIES

food served

music played

toasts and speeches

decorations

special memories

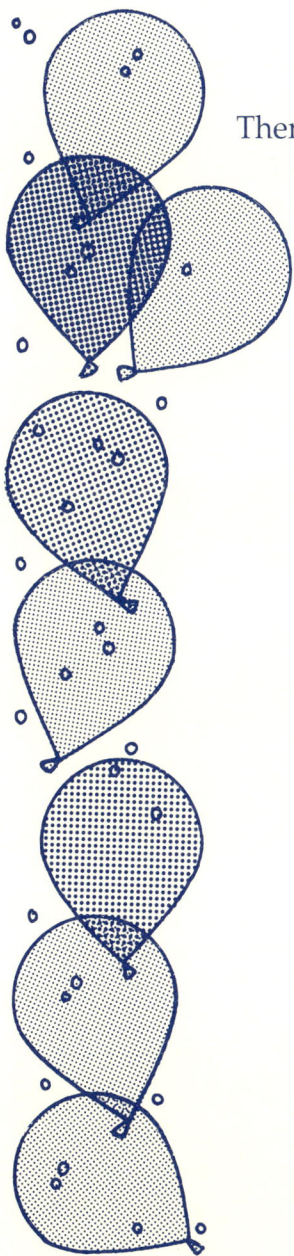

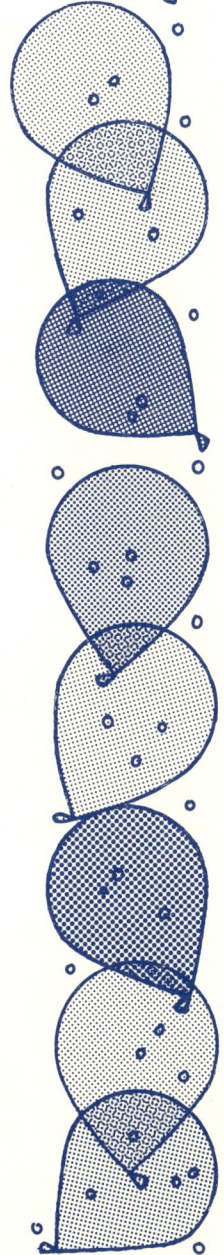

IN THE NEWS

On the day of my Bat/Bar Mitzvah, here's what made the news!

The headline on the front page

**Three important names
on the front page**

_____

_____

_____

**The topics of some articles
that interested me**

_____

_____

_____

_____

_____

_____

Who's Who?

President of the United States

_____

Vice President

_____

Secretary of State

_____

Supreme Court Chief Justice

_____

Governor of my state

_____

Senators from my state

_____

_____

What's the weather like? _____

_____

IN THE NEWS

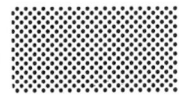

More things that happened on the day of my Bat/Bar Mitzvah

Three foreign countries making the headlines

_____

_____

_____

Three names in the sports pages

_____

_____

_____

On Wall Street

Here are the closing prices of the following stocks on

_____

month-day-year

AT&T   _____

The Gap   _____

Coca-Cola   _____

McDonalds   _____

PepsiCo   _____

Hershey   _____

WalMart   _____

The topic of an editorial or a letter to the editor

_____

_____

Title of a new movie being promoted

_____

Four advertised products and their prices

_____

_____

_____

_____

The names of my favorite comic strips

_____

_____

_____

HOW MUCH?

Here are the approximate prices of these items:

	at the time of my bat/bar mitzvah	five years later
a large cheese pizza	_____	_____
a loaf of bread	_____	_____
a haircut	_____	_____
a gallon of unleaded gas	_____	_____
a video rental	_____	_____
a student movie ticket	_____	_____
a compact disc	_____	_____
a rock concert ticket	_____	_____
a game of miniature golf	_____	_____
a game of bowling	_____	_____
a Sunday newspaper	_____	_____

NEW RESPONSIBILITIES

Now that I have become a Bat/Bar Mitzvah,
I will take on the following new responsibilities:

PERSONAL RESPONSIBILITIES

FAMILY RESPONSIBILITIES

RELIGIOUS RESPONSIBILITIES

HELPING OTHERS

When you become a Bat/Bar Mitzvah, you take on the obligation of *mitzvot* or helping others. Think of some creative ways you can use the occasion of your Bat/Bar Mitzvah to help others. Here are a few ideas:

Donate a percentage of the Bat/Bar Mitzvah money you receive to a charity or organization that is working to help others.

LITERACY CENTER

RED CROSS FIRST AID STATION

Day Care

Donate some of the money you receive to help plant trees in Israel.

For your reception, decorate your tables with baskets filled with canned goods. Donate the baskets of food to help feed people in need in your community.

Discuss these and other ideas with your family. Decide on a plan that works best for you. Put your plan into action and discover the feeling of satisfaction that comes from helping others.

THE SPIRIT OF MITZVOT

Here are some of the ways I want to help others:

in my home	at school

at my synagogue	in my community

other ways I can make a difference

FAST-FORWARDING INTO MY FUTURE

These computer screens depict my life as I would like it to be.

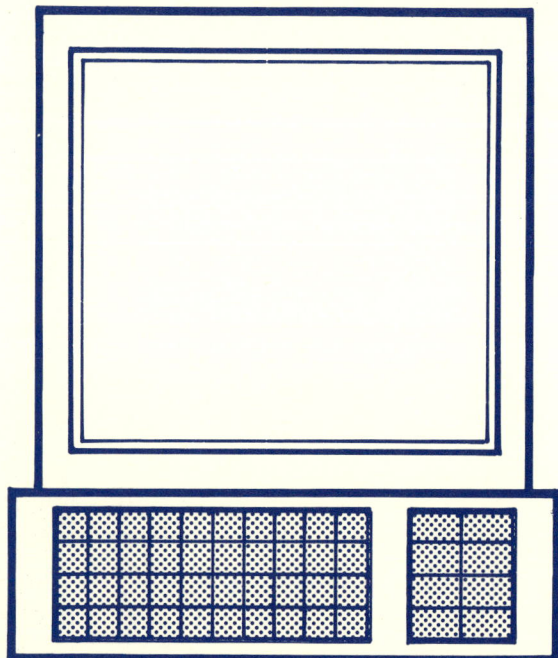

one year from now

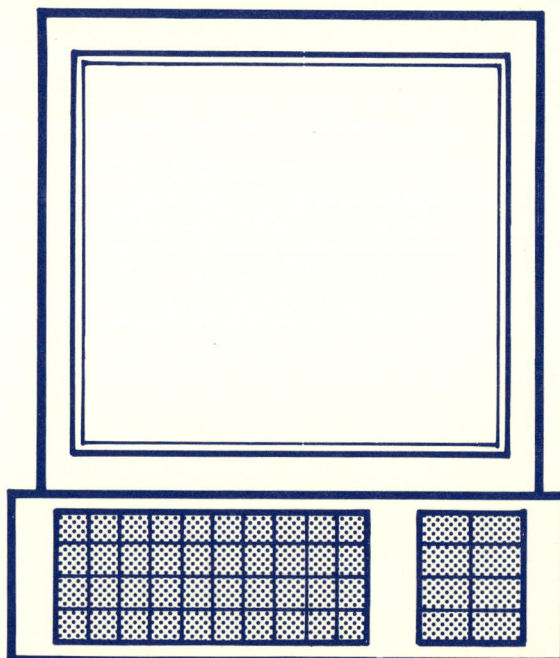

five years from now

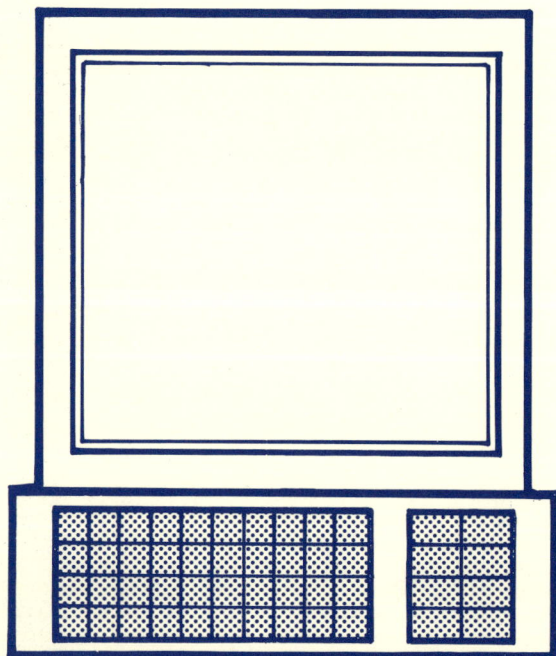

ten years from now

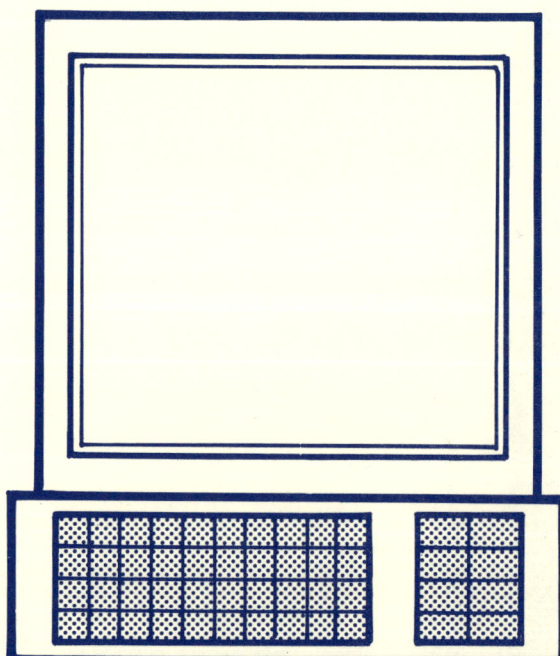

twenty years from now

A LETTER TO THE ME OF THE FUTURE

Think about the person you will be five years from now. What will your life be like? How will you have changed? If you could talk to "the you of the future," what would you say? Write out your thoughts and questions in a letter to yourself.

MY GOALS

I would like to become better at _____

_____

_____

A new hobby I'd like to try is _____

_____

At home, I'd like to _____

_____

At school, I'd like to improve in the area of _____

_____

I'd like to become better friends with_____

_____

One habit I'd like to try to change is_____

_____

A book I would like to read is _____

_____

Some very special goals of mine are _____

_____

_____

_____

MESSAGES FROM MY FAMILY

MESSAGES FROM MY RELATIVES

MESSAGES FROM MY RELATIVES

MESSAGES FROM MY FRIENDS

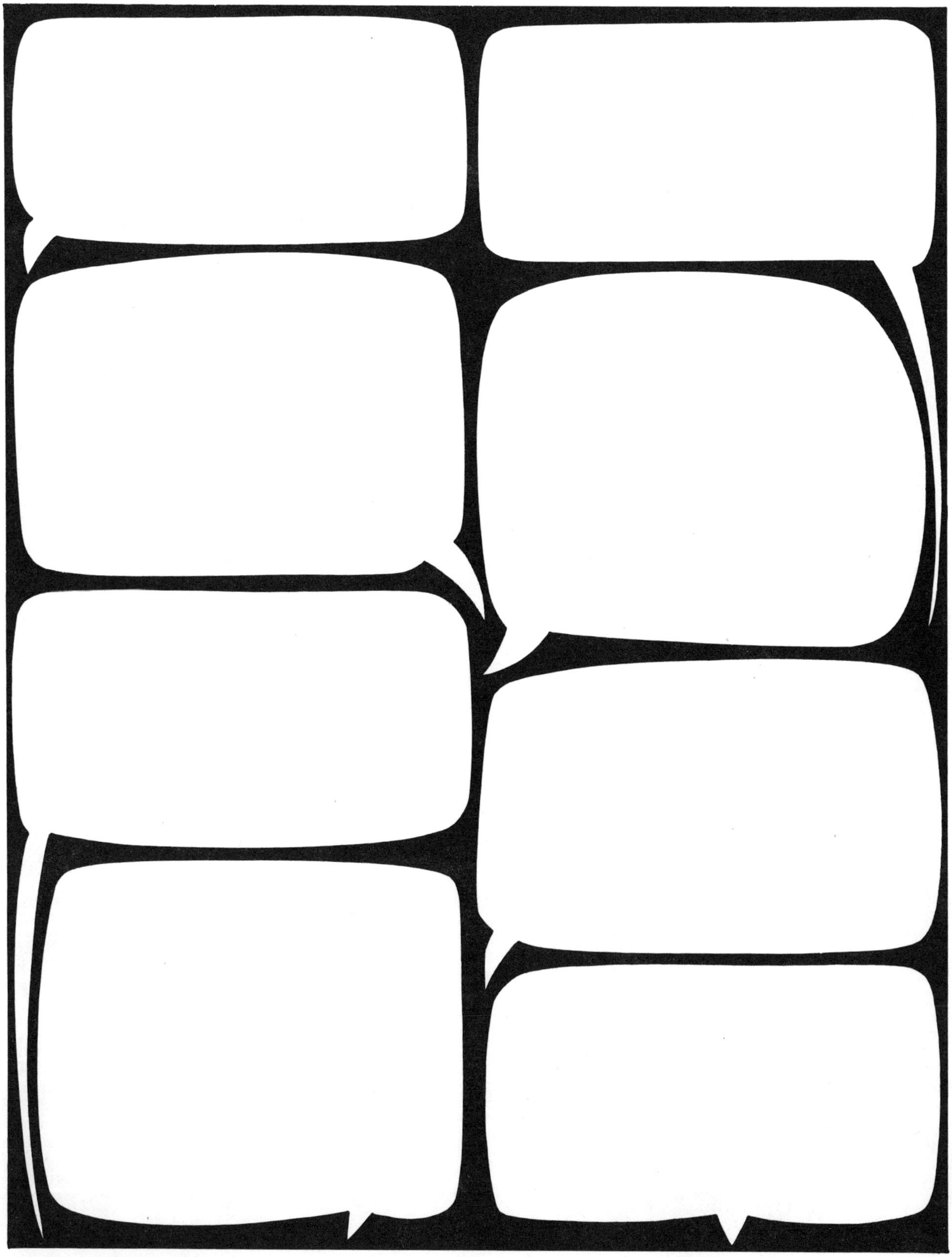

MESSAGES FROM MY FRIENDS

MORE MESSAGES!

MORE MESSAGES!

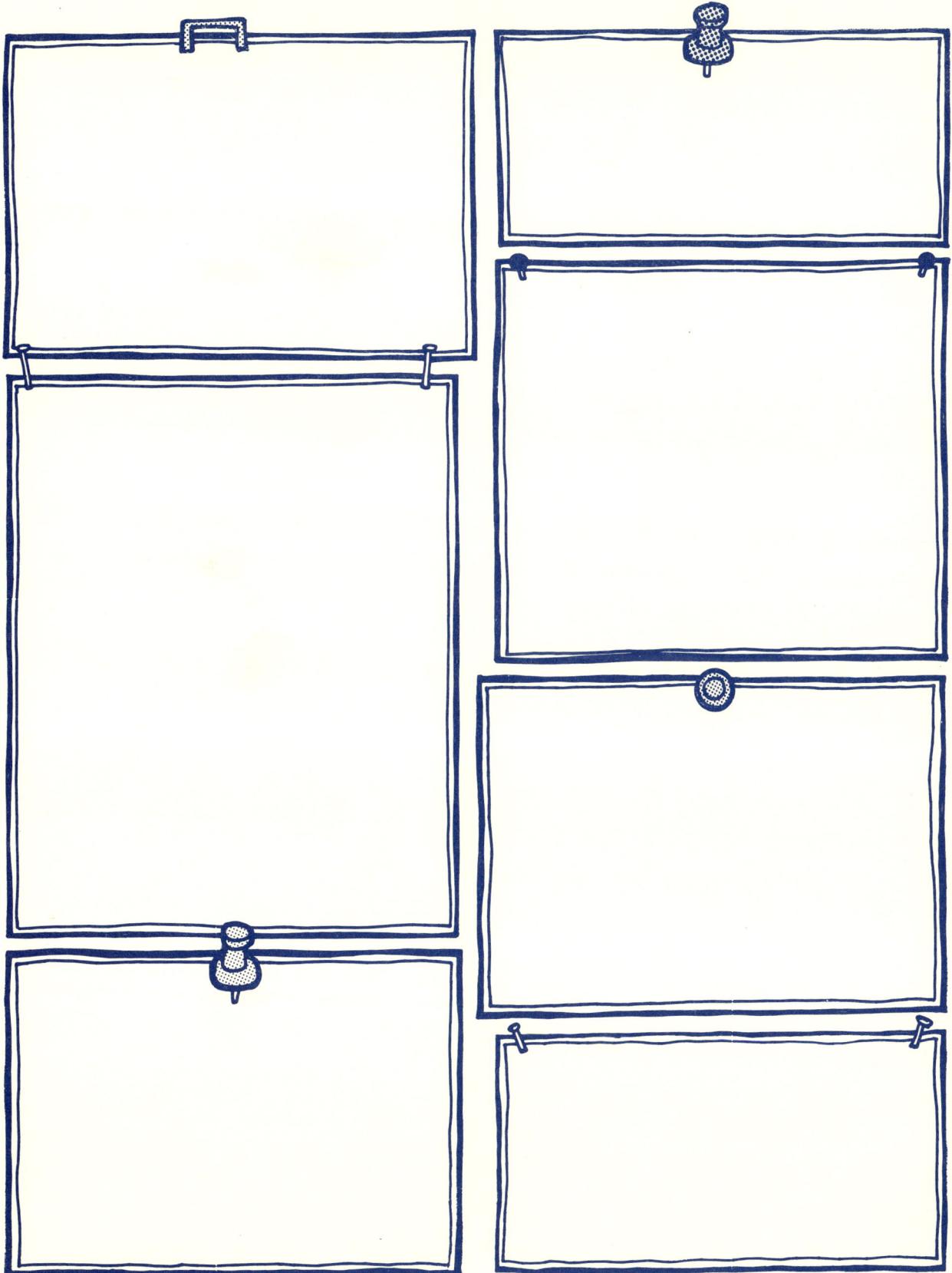

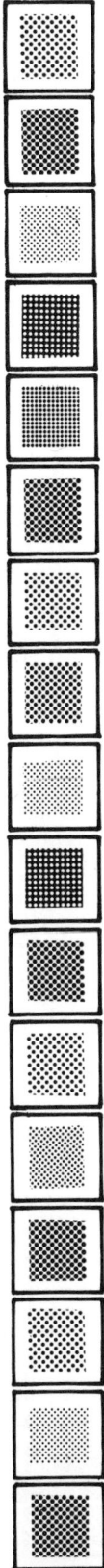

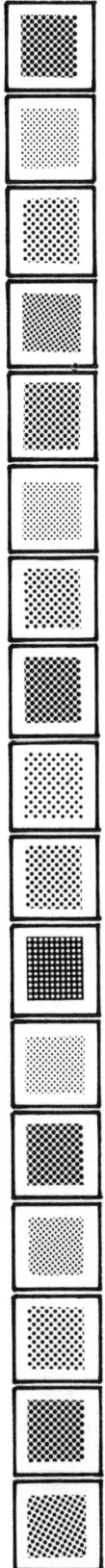

PHOTOGRAPHS

PHOTOGRAPHS

MEMORIES & MEMENTOS

MEMORIES & MEMENTOS

MEMORIES & MEMENTOS

MEMORIES & MEMENTOS

MEMORIES & MEMENTOS

MEMORIES & MEMENTOS

MEMORIES & MEMENTOS